# Fish
# Kite

**Bryan Rickert**

Copyright© 2018 Bryan Rickert
ISBN: 978-93-88125-44-4

First Edition: 2018
Rs. 200/-

Cyberwit.net
HIG 45 Kaushambi Kunj, Kalindipuram
Allahabad - 211011 (U.P.) India
http://www.cyberwit.net
Tel: +(91) 9415091004 +(91) (532) 2552257
E-mail: info@cyberwit.net

Printed at Repro India Limited.

# ACKNOWLEDGMENTS

I would like to extend my sincere thanks to the editors and publishers of the following journals in which many of these poems were originally published:

Modern Haiku, Akitsu Quarterly, Atoms of Haiku III, The Bamboo Hut, Failed Haiku, Acorn, Blithe Spirit, Prune Juice, Frogpond, Chrysanthemum, The Heron's Nest, Tinywords, Cattails, The Cicada's Cry, Shamrock, and ephemerae.

I would also like to thank Stephen Koritta for designing the book cover, Ben Moeller-Gaa for his haiku insight these many years and to my wife, Rita, for supporting me in all the other ways that matter so much.

# THE SMELL OF THE SEA

playing it
with a little more line
fish kite


first tilling
a plow parts
the crows


up to their knees in spring  egrets

after the storm
a rainbow rides
the hummingbird's throat


Ides of March
the mysterious way
birds turn as one

puddles
become Kandinskys
city rain


blossom viewing
a garden full
of selfies

the thin taste
of yesterday's tea
slow spring rain


the washline full
of sparrow song
Easter Sunday

the cloudburst ends
the wrenburst begins


baptizing
the moment
coffee steam

rain
one steeple
at a time


dandelions
the neighbors blow wishes
into my yard

summer sunrise
my daughter's voice
mixed with birdsong


pennies tossed
ripples from her wish
intersect mine

art class
the window fly
draws our attention


talking religion
the slipperiness
of mossy stones

last day of school
a cicada slowly
slips it's skin


between my hands and Venus fireflies


heat breaking rain
a cheer goes up
from the frogs

cicadas
double their efforts
Hiroshima Day


the lizard strikes
it's warrior pose
the heat!

country road
slipping back
into familiar trees


old homestead
lost to the waves
of prairie grass

summer heat
a snake in the hen house
lumpy with eggs


garden weeds
questioning my neighbor's
long term interests

magnolia blossoms
lingering in the heat
her last words


opening night
the conductor's shadow
embraces the stage

blossoms scattered
along the tarmac
a thousand goodbyes


beach vacation
the flat bottoms
of clouds


never the one you want nude beach

island breeze
every clothespin
line dancing


West Indies
the day comes
in waves

vacation's end
finding my worry stone
right where I left it


sand
from an old shell
my former self

summer's end
I unpack
the smell of the sea

# CICADA SHELLS

first date
the comfort
of old shoes


bar patio
the crass language
of crows

home late
the look I get
from the cat


wondering
what he sees in me
identity thief

ocean swim
the taste of salt
on her


she lets the garden go    miscarriage


a necklace
of clover blossoms
Mother's Day

undressing
a glimpse of the girl
she used to be


it's gentle caress in the night house fly


recycling
the death notice
buried deep

gumbo
the feel of mother's hand
in the old spoon


high school crush
all the what ifs
at the funeral

wondering
how things are back home
Edelweiss


reunion
a lobby full
of regrets

comfortable with our silence dappled rain


sculpture park
as I approach    the deer
become statues


Father's Day
an acorn dangles
from it's sprout

the slow lift
of morning fog
coffee steam


Get Well balloon
I finally learn
to let go

nursing home
the bent silhouette
of an old pine


after the gardener's death
the maple and pine
finally meet

late vigil
holding hands by the glow
of life support


the ritual
of a clean shave
funeral day

graveside
a cloud comes together
then disappears


cleaning father's closet
the shoes
I still can't fill

cicada shells
what to do
with the urn


reading the will
I inherit
the anxiety

moving day
the outline of a cross
left behind


cremation
to keep them from dancing
on my grave

# A DISTANT BLUE

visiting the place
I put your ashes
dogwoods in bloom

one last chance
to second guess myself
indian summer

August twilight
the cicada's cry turns
into frog song


night drive
between Mars and Venus
a way home

eating corn
in neat rows
the combine


country club
the arrogant strut
of a mallard

the length
of autumn
corn stubble


wearing
the teabag thin
mackerel sky

autumn storm
throwing caution tape
to the wind


for an hour
clouds graze the mountains
before passing

the start stop
of a stumbling leaf
rum punch moon


searching for enlightenment I find an app


autumn turns
the firm grip
of cockleburs

after the shooting
the absolute silence
of sunset


new winter
the dog runs through
it's exhale

frantic
in the headlights
first snow


winter rain
the blackbirds rise
against it

we take turns
holding the coffee
December


the flow
of bodies through it
city rain

long winter
the stray dog's shadow
grows thin


the mouse's neck
askew in the trap
seasonal depression

streetlight to streetlight
the moth
the beggar


daybreak
the junkie's
empty stare

winter night
the clarity of stars
in her eyes


one last fold
of the origami swan
night falls

for Johnny Baranski

Buddha
his little hat
of snow


dead of winter grandma's last preserves


coffee steam
curls back to the spoon
solstice night

midwinter
smell of the washrag
on every dish


New Year's Day
the hawk's long shadow
becomes mine

the long reach
of a sycamore's branch
winter sky

deep winter
whispering "come on baby"
while starting the car

filling it with tea  the emptiness

snow melt
finding the road
and walking it



snow on the blossoms
the magpie's call
a distant blue